Sunbathing on
Tyrone Power's Grave

SUNBATHING ON TYRONE POWER'S GRAVE

poems

Kim Dower

 Red Hen Press | *Pasadena, CA*

Book layout by Tessa Pechenik

Library of Congress Cataloging-in-Publication Data
Names: Dower, Kim, author.
Title: Sunbathing on Tyrone Power's grave : poems / Kim Dower.
Description: First edition. | Pasadena, CA : Red Hen Press, [2019]
Identifiers: LCCN 2018055874 | ISBN 9781597096218 (tradepaper)
Classification: LCC PS3604.O9395 A6 2019 | DDC 811/.6—dc23
LC record available at https://lccn.loc.gov/2018055874

The National Endowment for the Arts, the Los Angeles County Arts Commission,
the Ahmanson Foundation, the Dwight Stuart Youth Fund, the Max Factor Family
Foundation, the Pasadena Tournament of Roses Foundation, the Pasadena Arts &
Culture Commission and the City of Pasadena Cultural Affairs Division, the City of
Los Angeles Department of Cultural Affairs, the Audrey & Sydney Irmas Charitable
Foundation, the Kinder Morgan Foundation, the Meta & George Rosenberg Foun-
dation, the Allergan Foundation, and the Riordan Foundation all partially support
Red Hen Press.

First Edition
Published by Red Hen Press
www.redhen.org

Acknowledgments

Many thanks to the editors of the following journals and publications in which these poems first appeared:

The CDC Poetry Project, "I Am My Own Transgender Fetus"; *The Enchanting Verses Literary Review*, "Alternative Facts"; *Levure littéraire*, "Puzzle"; *Los Angeles Review*, "Happy Hour," "Lives," "Unruly Aura," "Naming the Puppy"; *Poem-a-Day, Academy of American Poets*, "He said I wrote about death,"; *Rattle*, "The Delivery Man"; "Letter to My Son"; *Santa Barbara Literary Journal*, "Late September"; *San Diego Reader*, "What it Means When You Dream You Bought a Red Cadillac," "Dogs and Poetry," "Dead Tired"; and *Solstice Magazine*, "Thirsty."

With heartfelt thanks and endless gratitude to my publishers, Kate Gale and Mark E. Cull, and to the devoted team at Red Hen Press.

And, to my Poetry Angel—forever and forever.

For Thomas Lux
poet, teacher, friend, like no other
in gratitude
you will never be forgotten

Contents

I

II

III

Sunbathing on
Tyrone Power's Grave

I

HE SAID I WROTE ABOUT DEATH,

and I didn't mean to, this was not
my intent. I meant to say how I loved
the birds, how watching them lift off
the branches, hearing their song
helps me get through the gray morning.
When I wrote about how they crash
into the small dark places that only birds
can fit through, layers of night sky, pipes
through drains, how I've seen them splayed
across gutters, piles of feathers stuck
together by dried blood, how once my car
ran over a sparrow, though I swerved,
the road was narrow, the bird not quick
enough, dragged it under my tire as I drove
to forget, bird disappearing part by part,
beak, slender feet, fretful, hot,
I did not mean to write about death,
but rather how when something dies
we remember who we love, and we
die a little too, we who are still breathing,
we who still have the energy to survive.

If you see a crib

by the side of the road, don't stop.
It's a trick and you will be robbed
or worse. They put cribs on the freeway
to entice us to pull over to help
the baby we think is there, but there is
no baby. If I saw a crib by the side of the road
I would inevitably stop because it could be real
and I could never sleep knowing
I might have saved a life even if mine
were in jeopardy, even if there were no baby
I would kiss the bare wicker where the infant
might have been, I would lift the imagined
girl or boy, hold it up to the sky
while they stripped me of everything—
cash in my pocket, silk jacket, last words—
they can have it all because maybe I
could have saved a baby, maybe this
is something I could have done, not for myself
but for a stranger, something that would matter,
like the moon matters to the night traveler,
like the sun matters to tomatoes, like the bees
matter to the white roses struggling in my backyard.

APPLIANCES

I love to turn them all on
sit in the kitchen
close my eyes
listen
to the music of machines
hear them do my work for me:
wash my clothes, clean my dishes,
dissolve my garbage.
I bought a lawn mower just to ride around in
hear its hum, pretend to trim the grass I don't have.
It smooth sailed over the concrete down the block
to the next street my Slow   Moving   Vehicle.
Where are the cows when you need one? Where
are the chickens? My toaster is my favorite appliance.
I can decide how to set it depending on my taste.
I like it medium to dark, brown enough so I know it's toast,
but not burnt. I don't like black flecks sprinkled across my plate.
I've never owned an electric knife. Too much margin for error.
My father never used one to carve the turkey.
Instead he used the knife he'd had since he got married,
right after the war. A wedding gift from some uncle
I never met. It was stainless steel and he sharpened it
religiously. I could see it shine from across the room.
Real cooks don't use electric knives, he'd say.
They make them better now—with batteries.
If he were alive, I might buy him one, just to try.
I would not tell him about my tractor
or talk about the cows.

Unruly Aura

The cashier at the health food store
tells me I have a beautiful aura.
Wait, I tell her, if you want to see
a really beautiful aura, wait until I've taken
my Renew Life Ultimate Flora Probiotic.
After that, my aura will knock your socks off.
She smiles at me and rings me up. My money
has a beautiful aura, too. My dollar bills
float out of my pink wallet. The man behind me
swells from the heat I generate. Each step I take
brings me closer to God, the final, fabulous aura.
Take my hand, I tell her, squeeze my aura—
it's hungry, and looking for someone to devour.

The Rockettes

Since I was a little girl
in pink taps, squeezing
my grandfather's hand
on the subway platform
waiting for the 7th Ave IRT
its thunderous screech
didn't unnerve me—
we were on our way
downtown to see
The Rockettes
Radio City
their glittering tiaras
their curtain of legs
rising, falling, rising,
sisters joined at the hip
not just as dancers
but protectors
of one another, of women,
their pointed toes, kicks
punctuating the air
taking care to dance for me
and all the other little girls
who looked up to them.
How great fifty years later
those legs are still swinging
freedom all over the stage,
legs that won't rise
for just anyone.

Thirst

My father never saw my house
though without his modest savings
we never could have bought it.

My father didn't know his grandson
past the age of ten, but today at 28
my boy has his eyes

and many of his talents. My father
died thirsty. We couldn't fill
his needs; no one could.

He had a big personality, my mother
would say, sucked the air
out of a room, needed you to pay

attention to his every word, a wall
of talk we wanted to jump over.
My father could tell a good

joke, do the accents, had the timing.
Why wasn't *that* appreciated.
He could sell anything, untangle a knot

out of the most delicate chain.
His stuff looked nice, his paintings framed.
He'd serve pats of butter on a dish

restaurant style. Our people leave us
and we let them go. They fade
into the tapestry of the dead,

an occasional memory slapping us
in the face tapping us on the shoulder
kissing the breeze by our cheek.

We wait for the wind to blow
these reminders, like it did for me today,
just now, in my garden that he never saw,

but would have loved, even though my roses
are struggling, their white petals dropping.
So thirsty they are; so ready for a drink.

How I Spent My Summer Vacation

We had to write these essays every September
about our adventures in faraway towns—
sleepaway camp, lakes, exotic birds, injuries—
sometimes we'd just make the stories up
because to be honest our summers sucked.
We'd hang inside the humidity of the city
stuff our faces with pizza, gulps of grape soda
but those reports needed to be filled
with *action words*, Ms. Larson told us,
so I made up that I found a deer in the woods
called him James, the insides of his ears
were bright turquoise, he let me ride him
by the river's edge, we sang Beatles songs.
I never took James to the city or showed him
the marble staircase where we spent all of August
scooping up jacks on the cold steps, bounced
that little red ball between sips of blackberry wine
lifted our dresses just enough, followed the man
from apartment 5C who never spoke to anyone
down to Riverside Park, and none of us would dare say
what we let him see, even though it was dark,
nor would we write about it in September
though we could have used a lot of colorful words
might have gotten an A, but you don't want to commit
to writing that which you'll spend a lifetime
pretending never happened.

WHAT IT MEANS WHEN YOU DREAM
YOU BOUGHT A RED CADILLAC

it means your face is on fire
it means your hands grab anything that moves
it means you want to be kissing her scarlet knees
it means you want one bloody shrieking crimson haunted wish
to finally come true as you speed past
your blindfolded childhood   drive until your life
finally works   it means you want a ride so fast so smooth you'll glide
into home right through your front door no questions asked
it means your inflamed dream is racing you into the future
where naked people are waiting to greet you embrace you
are lined up to jump inside the passenger seat
it means your headache will recede into a night of fingertips
easing the pain your back drenched against the leather
cherry colored ignition blush like your first hot wheeled crush
energy pulsing feet solid on the pedal touch
your hands 10 and 2 o'clock like they taught you back then when
all you cared about was her skirt riding up over your cool hand
slap her thigh it hurt to look her in the eye one kiss to last all summer

Family Wearing Pajamas Runs Across the Tennis Court in Plummer Park

They're holding hands, dressed in flannel.
The boy, around three, wears a one piece:
reindeers, candy canes in a zigzag pattern,
parents in plaid—mom red, dad blue—
boy has a hood, too. It's Christmas,
even in LA we're shivering.
They run across the court, balls flying fast,
players annoyed. Why not use the path,
why cross those lines into the face of danger,
but there they are, a family, fingers threaded,
laughing, lifting the boy into the air.

SHE'S NEVER TRUSTED HAPPINESS

Maybe it was something her mother said
one morning as the young girl dipped
her donut into a glass of whole milk
powdered sugar still on her lips her mother
tells her, don't get used to this

INK

I unscrew my fountain pen
a gift from a writer I
love—that deep ink kind of love
that can never be erased.
He tells me I need to remove
the cartridge before I board
the plane, tells me it will explode
if it remains locked in the pen,
like my heart sometimes feels
it's going to explode so confined
in my chest. This scares me, you see
because I'm not sure how to replace
the cartridge without breaking
the pen and I don't want to fuck
it up. I will try as hard as I can
to follow instructions and not
push too hard; I will try to un-
screw and re-screw and it should
all be fine. After all, it's just a pen,
albeit a pen that when I hold it
in my hand it appears that my hand
is dancing the words right onto the page,
the words circling back into my heart,
my heart pounding to get out.

I Can Always Tell When
Someone Makes a Good Snack

She's in front of me at the bank,
hair nestled on top of her head,
and I can tell this woman knows
what to put between two crackers.
I get hungry watching her,
not because she looks good to eat,
but because I can imagine her fingers
rolling dough into balls, powdered sugar
stuck to her knuckles. I can picture
the delicacies she'd load onto a tray,
serve to children in a circle on the floor,
or to me, in bed, recuperating from a sudden
illness for which there might not be a cure.
I've always found it hard to prepare
my own meals, long for someone else
to place my dinner on the table, someone
who asks for nothing in return.
Mothers will do that, fathers maybe,
siblings rarely because all they want
is what the other one has. This woman looks
like she has a bunch of sisters who all make
good snacks while they criticize one another's
children. They go on trips, giant coolers filled
with homemade breads packed tight in the trunk,
pâté to kill for. I envision this woman washing
her hands, lavender scented soap, before she readies
the roast for the oven, a prime rib she'll serve
to a silent husband.

TOWNIES

don't talk
as much as city boys
their arms are bigger
they can drive a stick
they don't care
about restaurants
or perfume
they like to do it
all the time
anywhere
they have things
they keep
in boxes, like old snake
skins or buttons
from swap meets
I loved one once
he liked to do it
in my parents'
summer cottage
when they were out
getting vegetables
he'd scoop me up
like a fireman saving
my life, toss me
on the calico print couch
damp with salt air
my ass burned
from rubbing

against the coarse fabric
he gave me a hickey
the size of a heart
I watched it fade
like the sunset
as I took the ferry
back home

LAX to FLL

It's 7:50 a.m. in LA I'm on my way
to LAX forgot to pack my hair dryer
who cares as long as I have my Xanax can't fly
without it though Brett my meditative friend
says try just once not to take it,
but I can't try today, want to zone out
listen to the pilot's voice, I think he said
his name is Gary, as the woman next to me
spills into my seat, chews something
with peanuts, keeps hitting me with her elbow,
I focus on Gary, on the clouds, as my mind blurs
did I close the gate, will my son pay his doctor's bill,
will my husband talk to himself the whole week I'm gone?
A child in the back of the plane shrieks.
I remember my son crying like that once,
had been awakened in the night, our neighbor
was mowing his lawn or starting his motorcycle,
it was something loud that woke my son, and we couldn't
console him, no milk, no holding, and this child
in the back of the plane continues screeching
as we lift above the clouds, as Gary tells us the headwinds
are good, we'll make good time, I like to hear *good* as I fly
as the Xanax releases through my blood as this child
screams needles out of his body, I wonder about
the neighbor who woke my son in Laurel Canyon
when we lived in paradise when none of us talked
to ourselves, and here's that elbow again jutting
into my rib, she's fallen asleep, so close I lean

into the window my mouth against the glass kissing
the clouds below, the clouds taking me to Florida,
Gary warning the turbulence is bound to come,
always comes, my roast beef on rye in my purse under
the seat, a sandwich I'll forget to eat, it's his ears,
I think, that poor kid's ears, why don't they give him
something to suck.

DAUGHTER SUSPECTS DEAD MOTHER
OF STEALING HER SHOES

My shoes are missing.
I looked on the bottom of my closet
and none are there. Not the boots
you loved me to wear, the ones that tied
up criss cross that always came undone,
not the simple black pumps I saved for work.
Did you take them? We can share, you know,
I'm fine with that, I loved the ones you wore
to the wedding, remember? Black patent
leather, simple bow. The red ones I never
liked. Ostentatious, Nana said.
People will see your shoes before they see
you, and what good is that?
I will leave the house now, my bare feet
poised for the cold or heat, my toes
digging in to the moist soil where I once
planted the pit from an avocado we had for lunch.
There was plenty of sun back there.
Something should have grown.

Puzzle

She solves puzzles all day
thirteen across: four letter word
for dying; one down:
phrase for love without limits
she wracks her brain
squeezes her eyes tight
she can taste the right word, ripe
ready to drop into her consciousness
under the table a bedazzled
dog rests his head on her naked toes
she'd wear slippers if she could find
the right pair—comfortable, not *too* soft
Ah! eleven across: "diced dish"
this has got to be "hash," she thinks
but it's one letter short:
the final insult
to another unsolved day

They gave him a manual

to reteach him how to tie his shoes
show him how to find the door
put his heart back together.

He could do nothing without her.
They told him this manual
with red leather covers, small enough

to slide into his back pocket
thin enough so no one would suspect
would walk him through the steps

of how to forget, how to dissolve
the despair that circles his air
like fine mist from pesticides.

He needs instructions on how to chew
a full bite of dinner, swallow
without it coming back up.

He dismisses this manual, thinks
it's like having a compass in a grave until he tries
Step One: close your eyes, see her face.

Step Two: climb into the boat you keep
by your bed. Step Three: row until your arms
feel as heavy as your heart, then drop

into the lake you've created with your tears
swim until the ache in your chest shatters
like knucklebones in battle.

He follows all directions.
He falls in love with the manual
and when they come to take it back

they are singing a song he heard as a child
did you ever hear tell of Sweet Betsy from Pike—
who crossed the wide prairie with her lover Ike

He is ready to let it go.
He's memorized all the steps he'll ever need
to take himself apart.

The Right Tool for the Job

You wouldn't use a steak knife
to butter toast, my father once told me
when I wasn't using a steak knife
to butter toast. Makes sense, Dad,
I said, putting down the hammer
I was slamming into a pushpin.
Something like this, he said,
doesn't need the weight of a hammer,
just press using your own thumb.
Oh, I said, you mean the one I sucked
until 7th grade when the principal
called home "advising" you
your 13-year-old daughter was sucking her thumb
in algebra and we had the family talk,
you and Mom sent me to someone,
a shrink, I think, my thumb sporting tiny
bite marks on both sides, nail bed mush
from my tongue's constant thrust.
My thumb was, for sure, the right tool
for *that* job, and kept other tools like reds,
Marlboros out of my mouth. Even today,
don't force it, I hear my father say,
like when I can't close the dishwasher
something's in the way and I push
the door, plates fall over on their sides,
glasses crack, *don't force it*, I hear his voice
as I keep pushing to make it work,
forcing another screw into that wrong-
sized deadbolt, always creating a hole
too large to fill.

In the Moment

I just parallel parked exactly right
for the first time ever. Maybe because
I wasn't imagining a tsunami
killing me on Sunday in Laguna,
or thinking about my mother alone
at home, or when I dropped the puppy
off the patio (she was fine; I never recovered).

Today, windows down, no radio,
just sky, steering wheel and my hands
were one, and backing into the space,
feeling my tires hug the curb, was a clean
slide into home. That rare fit of perfection
was upon me. And let me say right now,
I didn't waste it.

Everybody Loves Dinner

When I walk into my mother's house
I see a pot on the stove high flame

charring the sides
she thinks she's boiling

water but the water has evaporated
like a ghost fleeing the scene

leaving the bottom scalded, a blackness
that cannot be reversed.

It was only a matter of months. You see,
she was very careful in the kitchen

taught me the same:
check the pilot lights, smell for gas

unclutter the space where you cook
simple things like this she taught me

so last week when I visited when I saw
the blue flame hugging the sides of that old pot

sitting too close to the Kleenex I'd hand her
sobbing as she watched TV

so much violence, was it always like this,
sit down, darling, let's eat, everybody loves dinner

but there was no food, nothing there to cook
I hadn't brought a thing, what was I thinking

but we smiled, held hands, I changed the channel
she told me she felt full and was ready for bed.

The Echo of Love

They send me to the hospital
for an echocardiogram so they can see
inside my heart. Lou, the technician

tells me the heart is like a house
with many rooms and this will show them
the size of the rooms

if they have cracks in the ceiling, leaks
in the pipes, a damaged sun porch. I can hear
whooshing, see my blood flow

see it drop, the colors on the screen,
red, blue, green like a geyser exploding,
like the colors of falling in love, blasting

through my body, fluttering through the day,
same pounding, racing away,
my heart screaming let me out of here.

I say, Lou, how are things looking, pretty good,
huh? Big flow all those colors, and he says,
we need to take a deeper look before we know

if there's a problem. I understand. Look as deep
as you need, Lou. You will be the only one
who'll ever know what goes on inside those chambers.

THE MISUNDERSTOOD COLOR

You can't keep wearing pink forever,
he tells her. *It's the color of baby bonnets,*
stroller covers, satin bows that float down
the backs of feverish bridesmaids.
What you're saying is unfair to me, to pink,
to the world who sees pink as a warm ocean
they are waiting to step into, where they will bury
their swords and dance the pinkest dance
under a sky filled with savages.

THE BUNNY MOTHER

She was in charge of the club
in the Combat Zone,
handed us little suits
to pull up over our juicy
thighs—warm to the touch
from layers of clothes protecting us
from the wretched Boston winter—
no zipper just stretchy material,
coarseness I still remember.
The cups for our breasts
were sized to fit, but the body part
was one size fits all. It was a job
back in college—big tips, we'd heard—
glamorous, way better than The Pewter Pot
where I'd dropped a whole dinner,
ketchup and all, on a man's lap.
I'd be trading a chambermaid cap
for bunny ears, need only carry
a tray of drinks, bend over once in a while,
shake my bunny tail. We went, my friend
Shelly and I, for the audition. Open call
said the ad in the *Boston Globe*.
Bunny Mother wrapped the bow ties
around our necks, watched us walk in line
(I bought the spike heels at Filene's for $2.99),
watched us pretend to serve drinks to fake men.
I forgot to smile, was looking for the exit

of the dark hollow club buried beneath
the Pussycat Theatre. I remember the sweat
beads between my breasts sunk inside
their latex containers, Bunny Mother reaching
down my chest to lift them up, fill out the cup,
could hear my mother's voice, *stand up straight*,
my butt felt too big, and the tights they made us wear
had no crotch, just a hole to remind us.

COULD YOU LOVE *ME* MADLY?

I didn't understand "Light My Fire" but at fourteen could feel it was
nasty not what we New York kids slow danced to at our 8th grade par-
ties: "Save Your Heart for Me" was so Yesterday. The time to hesitate
wasn't through, but I sure wanted to try to set the night on fire when
Dino from Phil's Pizza gave me that look as he handed me a slice,
touched my lips with his fingers I was sipping grape soda, came in that
white cone shaped paper cup, my tongue purple as a *deep blue dream*,
my teeth biting the edges raw, my sunburned thighs mother's warn-
ings, brother's guitar, boyfriend's Timex slipping off my wrist the end
of sanitary pads, bring on the Tampax, bellbottoms, miniskirts, black
eyeliner and coming home last day of school before vacation, there
was Janet's mother splattered on the steaming sidewalk in front of our
building dressed up in a white lace skirt, blouse, lady gloves, we were
walking down 89th Street could see the chalk lines etched around her
body she had four children—the family from LA—we called them,
dad in the music business, she jumped from her 10th floor living room
window *Riders on the Storm into this life we're born, into this world
we're thrown*, Janet's mother dead, her kids huddled behind the yellow
tape, *you know the day destroys the night, night divides the day*, next
morning I left for LA, summer of love, teen tour, campers on an over-
night train, first stop Chicago pushing our bodies into every sunset on
our way out west, tee-shirts tight across our chests, summer
of *Valley of the Dolls*, desert heat all of us in the moment

as the moment was making history, when I saw his name on the marquee of the Whiskey my heart jumped out of the tour bus—could he love *me* madly? I would let him eat every secret I had right out of my mouth Jim Morrison was the darkness I wanted to get lost in *Don't you love her madly want to be her daddy don't you love her as she's walking out the door* Stop Children what's that sound *Come on, baby, take a chance with us and meet me at the back of the blue bus . . .* one pill makes you larger and one pill makes you small go ask any of us drowning diet pills with diet coke diet crackers, diet vomit, could music save our very souls as parents were dropping out of windows Riots on Sunset and back home, we too were blasting the Byrds, yes Something's Happening Here There and Everywhere we were turning on our love lights Jim Morrison I'd have kissed you loud enough to wake the dead that summer when we ironed our hair in a little motel facing the Hollywood Hills miles away from the dreary city where our mothers were killing themselves angels in white lace, wrong time wrong place *you know that I would be untrue you know that I would be a liar . . . can you see that I am not afraid—what was that promise that you made? This is the end, beautiful friend. This is the end my only friend.*

And all the children are insane, the children are insane, waiting for the summer rain.

II

Naming the Puppy

They're young and in love
so they think of human names:
Zoe, Ruby, Judy—like the name
of a girl you'd sit next to in math.
They move on to dog baby names:
Lamby, Girl, Puppy.
They like Puppy so for an hour,
that's what she's called.
Come here, Puppy, they sing,
her paws—pink, tender—slide
across the room. Puppy's a sweet name,
I tell them, but soon your puppy
won't be a puppy, and when she hurtles
through the park her teeth locked
onto a sloppy stick, a pit bull chasing her down,
how'll it sound when you call, *Puppy, Puppy,*
your voices airy as frisbees floating
across the grass. I watch the puppy lick
my son's lips, nibble his girlfriend's nose,
devour their faces, as if they were made of sugar,
devoted furball all ears and eyes,
eyes that have been on this earth before.
By dinnertime her name is Gwen,
a star's name, a nurse's, or what you'd call
the middle child of a noisy family.
I watch Gwen pour herself
into their arms. There is no name
for the way she loves them.
No name for a sun that shines only for you.

IF YOU GIVE A MOUSE A MANTRA

If you give a mouse a mantra
it will want a tiny cushion

If you give a mouse a tiny cushion
it will want a cute mouse to sit beside

If you give a mouse a cute mouse
it will not meditate but rather dissolve

into giddiness (as two mice will do)
and you will wake to dozens of baby mice

snoozing in your shoe. The takeaway?
Do not give in to the mouse's request

but rather suggest it inhabit the cushion
alone, concentrate on squeaking out its Om,

teach it how to inhale through its twitching
nose, fill its belly with a small puff of air, release

through its mouth—size of an infant's fingernail
forget about being chased by the cat

ready to attack, jealous you haven't given *her*
a mantra or tiny cushion. The cat is always

watching. Listen for the sound of her brain
changing; watch her pounce. See your mouse

swallow its mantra. See the cushion transform
into a confetti of Emptiness.

Dogs and Poetry

Last night I dreamed dogs were giving a reading
in my living room—long-haired, handsome, golden
and chocolate, tea cup poodles, a mix or two—
panting, stacked on a loft, pouncing one at a time
onto center stage couch, poems wet in their teeth—
collies on edge, pugs in love, shepherds fierce
with loyalty, labs with their hot heads in my lap.
I was sitting with them, coaching, petting, biscuits
by my side, rewards for their poems (mostly about love!)
which astonished the audience—a miracle, so fresh,
original, they barked in iambic pentameter, singing
the blues these dogs were so damn cool we all wanted
to nibble their pink bellies, suck life into our tired souls.

The Secret Afterlife of Bees

There's a seventy pound beehive
deep inside a wall of my house.
Bees flow in and out the window,
a swarm of breeze dancing
throughout the day.
We must get rid of them.
Gas them or do it the *humane* way:
cut into the wall, suck them into a vacuum,
release them, miles away, into a stranger's hive.
My mother used to cover her ears
with her hands when a bee buzzed by.
It could get inside your brain and die,
she told me when I was five.
A bee followed me down the street today.
We want to come out alive, she told me.
Do you know why bees die after they sting?
Massive abdominal ruptures. The impact
blows open their stomachs, like a gunshot.
In the secret afterlife of bees there are markings
on the trees: *We had no idea it would kill us,*
no idea we were risking our lives.

LIVES

I was never a gerbil
poodle or lizard
I was no one's wife
yet I carry in my bones
the memory of giving birth
in another century
under an orange moon
I always took a human form
in rags or gingham once in lace
imported from France
played violin in a king's
private chamber he
banished me
when I struck the wrong note
I have learned to cope
one life to the next
the ancient voice inside
corrupting and consoling
tells me I am here
to prepare meals for anyone
who's hungry I'm grateful
to crawl on all fours
carry a mouse in my mouth
hear it sing to its lover
who lives in the dark cottage below
where I was born many lives ago
in a room so silent I could hear my braids
grow each strand of hair a song
for my next life

Gwen is Scared of the Wooden Fish

She's a puppy, gets confused by objects
that stare but do not move. The wooden fish
painted yellow, blue, green, with a pink fish
painted in the middle leaning against
the orange dining room wall, for example,
we bought it long ago, one summer roadside,
Mexican border, a man with his own dog
made them, sold them to tourists heading home.
We've always loved the fish, the way it's carved,
the way it continues to balance on
the hardwood floor. Gwen pushes it with her
nose, licks it like it's her baby, looks at me
as if to say, why doesn't it have a tongue
why isn't this thing kissing me back? She jumps
away each time it doesn't move. We re-
assure her it's okay, this wooden fish
that fills us with memories.

Progress

Upstairs in the room
where my son used to live
I hear a stampede of animals
charging the roof, right above
where his head used to be.
I hear so many of them, God knows
what they are: squirrels, elephants, rats
for sure. He'd be scared up there,
that's what he said, and now I know why.
I worry these creatures might crawl
through the open windows, getting
louder overhead as I lay on the bed
like he did trying to fall asleep
after a long day at school, football,
the things they do we can never really
understand. I'm listening to my neighbor
talk on the phone; can hear his side
of the conversation, her side, too,
seems so intrusive but I can't stop
and probably my son listened, too, heard
the old married couple who moved away,
used to get high, sing old songs at the piano,
what did he think of them—were they a comfort
or a freak show, a window into what his parents
might become. I don't remember thinking anything
when I was fourteen except when can I
get out of here, as I studied my mother,

her friends, how they moved their mouths,
how their lips would curl down
when they spoke of their husbands.
This is what we do. This is the only way
we can understand our own species, shake
the dead off our bodies, invite ourselves
into the new world of ourselves.

It's So Hot, I'm Getting Stupid

It's so hot, I just opened a can of tuna
with my teeth. I forgot there were can openers
was surprised to taste the fish oil mingling
with my blood, open cuts on my lips and mouth.
We'll do things under extreme conditions: step inside
of horses when we're freezing, fall in love with murderers.
I would kill for you, I tell my children. And, I would.
I have made bad decisions today in the heat.
I climbed the pole outside my window hoping
for a breeze. When I fell onto the moving car
the driver and I locked eyes before I tumbled off.
I am not dead. I am having lunch. A bowl of cream.
The driver is traveling north, strands of my hair
plastered onto his windshield.

MOURNING

Every time a piece of food
drops on the floor, I brace
for my cockapoo to race

screeching nails slide
across wooden floors, rush
to slurp up the fallen crumbs.

But there is no dog.
Not anymore.
My feet, under the kitchen table

no longer rest on his back
toes buried inside his fur
now have no place to go.

He's not here to jump up
when I sneeze or to growl
at invisible intruders.

I thought I was used to his
being gone, but every time
I walk through my front door

I'm still careful not to step on him:
my phantom greeter
and I bend down to pet

a memory.

A KINDER DEATH

I picked a piece of lint
off the bedroom rug
or thought I did,
until the lint flit across my palm.
I flicked it back onto the rug,
ran to get a Dixie cup
but the spider refused
to crawl inside
had to push it, slide it
down the waxy side,
open my front door,
fling it onto the porch.
That night I couldn't sleep.
Where did it go?
Does its family know?
What if they're living
underneath my desk
weaving a silken tent
around an old box of letters,
waiting for their daddy
to come home, spin a web,
help them with their spider
homework. I should have
dumped it in the sink
to join the other insects

swimming down the pipes
in our toothpaste and spit.
Or better yet
I should have crushed it
right there on the rug
rather than force it into a world
of idiot squirrels.

CONFESSIONS OF A BUTTERFLY

I stuffed myself with milkweed
in my adorable larva stage
making my wings large

bright orange. I'm desperate
for people to admire
my delicate beauty and believe

I bring them good luck.
With my life span as short
as a rose's, I don't waste my time

fluttering through fields
mingling with flowers.
I plan to follow the heat, echo

in its warmth, power straight
into the sun, feel each ray slash
my wings, burn them to powder,

light up the world.

COOPER'S HAWKS

The drought brought the Cooper's hawks
who perch on high branches in smog-hazy air,
swoop down target hummingbirds, finch,
mourning doves, an explosion of feathers, sticky
with bird murder, fragrance of bones, drops
of sugar water fresh on their beaks. Yesterday's
freak summer shower sent the hawks away
and the little birds returned for a day, safe
from the blue darter predators, their hungry shrieks
replaced by the thirsty music of tree sparrows,
their open mouths questions I can't answer. They
trusted the feeder, their slow drip heroin swinging
in the breeze. When the hawks flew off we could hear
the earth groan. This newly parched world confuses the lizard.
I see him hiding under the fig tree. I watch as he counts
backwards to sleep, closes one eye, refuses to die.

BEE STING

I've heard it said
that when you get a bee sting
it means you will gain new insight.

When I got stung, minding my own business
sitting on the warm sand, all I felt was an ember
burning a hole in my back, a frantic itch

I couldn't reach. I ran to the lifeguard,
crying for him to remove the stinger,
he told me never touch, use a credit card

to scrape the venom off, one brisk move,
eradicate the barb, be certain to get it all
or the poison might spread into your head

where the insight is supposed to go instead.
To this day, part of the stinger remains
lodged under my shoulder blade.

The hallucinations vary. Right now I'm on a boat
sailing backward, all of us on deck lounging, nursing drinks,
lemon wedges swarming with bees, all of us singing songs

with long words, wearing colorful bathing suits,
on our way to meet the Queen who rules beyond
this life, in the forgiving hive of our future.

GWEN IS SCARED OF THE LEMON

I can't find a ball
so I grab a lemon from our tree.
It's round, it rolls, it even
smells like pee, bright yellow
glows in the sun as it shimmies
through grass and dirt
in her paradise backyard.
She catches it in her teeth
oozes out bitter, no treat, and now
she's confused, what's this thing
that squirts, a world of doubt
for a mouth that's never tasted
what we humans squeeze on fish.
She backs off, growls, barks in frustration,
smacks it with her paw,
licks it, pushes it with her nose,
bites its face off
won't let me take it away.
It's her lemon now
and there's nothing left of it to throw.
I'm ashamed I tried to fool her this way.
I was trying to please her in the moment,
by pretending one thing was as good
as something else. We all do it, don't we?
Tofu is not meat.
Those are not the kisses
that make your heart beat.

Risk

no one's ever stolen
the moon for me
hoisted it out of the sky

carried it on his back
rolled it across his shoulders
its cold white fumes

blasting him through space
stars sprawled out like clues
under his feet oh no one's

ever dared steal the moon for me
until you who sifted through
dirty clouds flew faster higher

than the hungry birds gnawing
the air their wings askew
believing the moon was theirs

Love Hurts

You are my tourniquet my Saturday
matinee my jelly bean storm pointer
and thumb you are my hidden door my home
is your skin you are the dream I taste the
moment I awake the bruised crime I live
to commit my drawbridge thunder shudder
you are my pink cloth childhood coat with
the velvet collar the red mark on my
arm the tunnel I crawl through on my hands
and knees the flapping bird struggling to fly

Anybody's Animal

I like to watch dogs lick the ears
of kittens, pigs protecting lambs,
baby squirrels being nursed by a cat.

Orphan animals being raised by mothers
of a different species makes me feel calm,
safe, makes me wish I was an animal, too,

a little white poodle being raised
by a heavyset kangaroo. Of course, I *am*
an animal, but the kind who makes things

complicated, wears deodorant, watches the news.
Though I've licked the ears of other mammals
I didn't love doing it like these boxers and goats.

I envy the relationship the baboon and bush baby
have. Even when no one's looking
they're nice to one another. I'm disguised

as a rescue hoping to be found in an alley.
I have no words, just the scent of my desire.
I am ready to be anybody's animal.

I Am My Own Transgender Fetus

My mother thought I was a lesbian
when I came home from college
wearing a flannel shirt fresh from a march
across the Boston Common, the '70s
no entitlement back then, no transgender
friend, we all hid inside our sleepless nights
smoking fat joints of science-based conclusions
rolling out our private stomach aches watching
evidence stack up higher than we could see.
I feel so vulnerable tonight, hungry for diversity—
where is my entitlement—I am my own
transgender fetus floating in a tank with no borders
banging my soft unformed skull into the glass ceiling
seeking any spray of light as our world rolls backward
over a grassless hill of mutant crickets button up
your collar until your mouth is invisible all evidence-based
science-based beautiful womb-faced lips erased
who doesn't crave a chance to say banned words
hear their echo like vapor stain the wall of our lives
our slurred speech aching for clarity.

III

Alternative Facts

The sky is blue because that's the color
my child likes to draw it. Two plus two,
if one of the twos is pregnant, equals five.
The earth is flat. Columbus, a fabulous guy,
fell off the side. He was also a loser
who didn't build a wall to protect
himself. The saleslady with a pencil
stuck in her bun caught me *borrowing*
bell bottom jeans at Morris Brothers
when I was thirteen. We do not all bleed.
In fact, blood is not always blood red.
Blood is a different color in different colored
bodies. I'm telling you and so it's true.
Facts only work when we need them to.
Take this knife and jab it into my guts.
Columbus is still inside me
discovering America.

SHOPLIFTING

The guard at CVS is having a conversation
with himself, using his hands to punctuate
answers to imaginary questions.
This might be a good time to pocket
the lip gloss, while he's so involved in making
his point. I nod at him, *how's it going*,
but he's too absorbed talking to no one.
At this rate I could steal more than just a gloss,
so I go for the small but expensive moisturizer—
the one they usually keep locked up behind the glass.
I wonder if it's less greasy than what I use at home—
wonder if it would make my skin more dewy and youthful.
The guard loves whomever he's not really talking to.
I grab the cream—stick it in my purse.
I have money, just want some excitement,
haven't stolen anything since junior high.
My heart doesn't race like it did back then—
not getting that energy-high, rosy-cheeked thrill.
Maybe I should up the stakes and try stealing something
that can't be concealed. What about that pink chaise lounge?
I check for a sensor. Nothing. Not even a price tag.
This is my moment. I walk past the guard, still entranced
with the voices in his head. I'm embarrassed to say
it was easy. I often wonder about the guard
when I lie in the chair in my backyard
where I've confined myself for the rest of my life,
my skin glowing.

THE DELIVERY MAN

would drive his little van down the street,
slide open the door, his face obscured
by hanging clothes draped in plastic bags,
take out his penis and masturbate
as he watched us play handball against
the Party Cake wall. We were nine or ten
maybe eleven and we knew when he drove by
what it would mean. Some of us stopped to watch,
could only see the quick movement of his hand,
but once I saw it all. It was like being transfixed
by a crash on the side of the road—ashamed
to want to take in the suffering of others, yet
bewitched by the horrifying images.
His grunts were obscured by the traffic,
but if you went close enough to his truck
you could hear the groan of relief when he was done.
He wore an oversized raincoat just like the joke.
We never told our dads but our moms knew.
They saw him, too. He's *exposing* himself,
my mother explained. No one made me look
but I couldn't turn away—paralyzed by fear
and the excitement of repulsion—of knowing
it was wrong but needing to see how he
did this thing, wanting to be his audience
in a sticky white mess of daylight.

HAPPY HOUR

Magicians never move away from their magic
the stranger in the bar tells me.
I'm waiting for my friend, sipping vodka
from two skinny straws. *They hover around objects*
that easily move, have special coins in their
pockets, face hair in unique places. Why
do you know so much about magicians,
I ask him? Are *you* a magician? *I wish,* he answers.
I'd change this room into a palace, we'd be dressed
in robes, layers of fabric draped around our ankles,
we'd be drinking ale and eating turkey legs,
laughing from our guts. We'd be dead
in the morning from poisoned apples—a dessert
prepared by the rival palace. Who *are* you?
I ask him, moving my drink closer to myself.
I am the heir to the throne in the village
where you were born, the one your parents
escaped from before you could walk. I'm the one
who saved you by hiding you in the sleeping car
on the train we're still riding.

Divers Search Lake for Killers' Secrets

What will they find?
An heirloom watch, rose gold, engraved
you're the one, a tiny hole where the ruby
used to be. And of his, not much.
The hammer that may have done
their victim in, though maybe it was hers.
They killed together, not for money
or revenge, for the thrill of surprise:
how far would they go, how much
could they stand to watch the other do?
Risk? Of course. They'd been married a long time.
But the lake looked clean and inviting,
the divers said, as they immersed
themselves in a world of pike and trout,
deep down leaves rooted in sediment,
no evidence. What *did* they find?
A man who'd been dead for years,
his face two dark holes where his eyes
used to be—not the couple's secret
but someone else's. *The lakes under the waves*
have waves of their own.

MARG

She told me she didn't know
who Marlon Brando was.
Call waiting confused her,
but she could speak eloquently
about the Incas, Chopin's
Nocturnes, how to caramelize
dates. Marg was one note
though Margaret, like a dance,
a sonata, was her given name.
She had a ready laugh, knew
what was funny, not a joke maker
but a joke taker, her face welling up
with all the laughter in the room
tears spilling from her eyes
laughing after the others had stopped.
She got it. She knew. She loved
her dogs, her house. These are only
some things to say about Marg.
She was always kind to me,
her eyes bright and listening.
She surprised us all.

EAVESDROPPING ON HER NEIGHBORS

What's the difference between a hurricane
and a tornado, she hears the wife ask her husband.
The man doesn't know the difference, and after a pause
tells her this: There *is* no difference. They both come
with strong winds, destroy property, homes.
They both can kill. She's not satisfied by his answer:
but what's the *difference*, she asks.
I told you, he says. Why do you keep asking?

ACCOMPLISHMENT

All I could do this morning
was change purses
retire spring summer
for fall winter
pull out my wallet, keys
ravished Q-tips, tissues
dried with last season's
snot, mystery hard candy
from Chi Dynasty
my dead father's money clip
that I carry for good luck
though it never brought him any
pull it all out, set it aside.
I will cram the out of season
pink and purple daisy dotted
handbag into the back of my closet
to discover next April
when I will do the reverse—
switch back, toss memories
I've yet to have, ones I will vaguely
remember from shorter days to come,
when the sky darkens at the end
of a long lunch—a ticket
from a museum in New York I've yet to visit,
a red crayon I won't recall, a matchbook
from that restaurant we don't love,
but always return to. I think we were there
last November—that place with the salty
garlic almonds. We got there before the first
snowfall, in a city where snow never falls.

DUBONNET

My grandmother would sip a juice glass
of Dubonnet—dark purplish red, color
of her identical twin sister's lips, the one
who stayed behind in Russia—every night
as she prepared the roast, Mike Douglas
blasting on the television, my grandfather snoring,
the apartment a swirl of garlic, chicken fat,
boiled secrets, longing flooding the rooms
like sunlight. Once she offered me a taste:
Some people like it with a twist of lemon,
but I like it plain. I was seven. My tongue burned
through the sweetness. I floated into the next room
without moving. I would dress up in her black
cloth cape, sequined ladybug pin, clump around
in her tiny pumps. She was the size of Thumbelina.
I remember the warm baths, splashes of Jean Nate,
the pink chenille bathrobe, photo of them as girls
hanging in the dark hallway. My grandmother
told me her name just once: "Tanya," this identical her,
living on the other side of the world, another Nana
saying goodnight to another me.

MAKING COFFEE

It annoys my guests
that I don't measure my coffee.
I "eyeball it," I tell them,
shake enough grounds
into the filter until it looks right.
They don't like it.
My family, friends, even house guests
feel the need to question, admonish,
even before they've had a taste,
they know it won't be right.
"Wait," I tell them, you'll see.
It'll be as good a cup of coffee
as any you've ever sipped.
After it's dripped, poured, with or without
the milk they want or don't want,
they're almost disappointed by its perfection,
mad at me for the rest of the morning,
until their annoyance fades into an afternoon
of questioning other things that don't add up:
"Why do *my* flowers die when I water them
exactly according to directions?"
"How could he lie and get away with it?"
"How is it she jumped from the cliff
and survived?"

BERRY & BARRIS

Chuck Berry, Chuck Barris
did they plan to die
the very same week?
Imagine the confusion in heaven
where everyone sits around
watching *The Dating Game*
as "You Never Can Tell" blasts
out of every cherub's transistor.
Barris running numbers, Berry
stringing guitars for saints,
everyone swapping stories
about one Chuck or the other,
both of whom are madly in love
with the same twisted angel

MAKER'S MARK

She knows what she likes
sends it back when it arrives
with too much ice, tells the waiter
this is not a real drink.
He knows she's right,
takes it away
two green olives, color of her eyes
like earrings she might wear
with a smart sweater
strung together
by a plastic sword.
She used to be my shrink
heard almost everything I'd think
knew me before I knew myself.
Retired now she's become my friend,
we go out for dinner, I'm secretly giddy
to be with her this way, her voice
a part of me, etched into my memory.
I can vaguely remember all those years
sitting across from her on that itchy beige couch
my legs tucked safely underneath me, her face
absorbing the stain of my life:
panic attacks in Bloomingdale's dressing room,
imagined fires, evacuations, phantom amputations,
tidal waves—in and out of the same revolving door
sticky with angst, year after year, what *is it* you fear,
and now we're here, *she's out of the business,*

my head still not clear, yet silent as the morning
after a blizzard, anxiety a muffled whisper,
faded like dried blood on a forgotten nightgown,
my problems like old clothes:
washed, softened, folded in a special drawer,
not ready to give away
but never to be put on again.

ROUTINE PHYSICAL

I pee into a little plastic cup
write my name on it with a crayon.
The doctor taps my knee with her silly
rubber hammer, sticks an icy steel light
into the dark hallway of my eardrum.
She listens to me breathe, asks,
Has anything changed—appetite, diet,
sleep pattern, partners? I will lie to her
as she probes my stomach with her
excellent hands, tell her there's a man
living inside the lower chamber of my heart
hiding inside a valve. She will instruct her nurse,
Maria, to press cold round discs onto my breasts
connect me to the machine. She will take
my blood, vial after vial and I will look away
knowing whatever they find will kill me
too slowly to matter. My blood is where
my secrets live. The man inside me whispers:
on your way out, grab some wet-naps
from the basket on the back of the toilet.
Get enough for me. I want to know what they feel like.

CONVERSATION WITH A STRANGER

for Baudelaire

"More people should rent," the stranger at the bar says. "Why?" she asks. "What do you mean?" "Because, to own is to die . . . to have something forever is to never let things change." "What do you mean?" she asks—"Tomorrow morning the bird on the roof will be gone before you get out of the shower. He will fly to another roof and you'll never see him. You won't know there ever was a bird on the roof." "Exactly," he says. "Except for feathers. There will always be the feathers. Sometimes feathers are everything."

Slib

Sounds like another word
for stone: that hard wall you hit
when you dig up your garden,
or the word for what might crawl
out from under the moist soil; or
Slib: noun, the hardened gristle
on an overcooked steak.
But slib is the Czech word
for promise—vow, pledge
sounds so glib, for something
so serious, but promises, we say,
are made to be broken
and maybe over there it's *really*
true: I slib to love you forever;
I slib to always stay. In Bohemia
our slib is our word.
Have a nice day.

DEAD TIRED

When you're tired
everything's worse.

Glimpsing a rogue hair
spurting from the side

of your chin is like seeing
the end of the world.

Have a nap your inner voice
instructs you, *have one now*,

lay down and float into the cloud
of dreams you should have had

last night when the heat
kept you tossing with worry

about people you love but can't
help, can't fix, if only they'd listen,

but you're too tired to grouse
so you dance naked

through the house, singing
loud enough to wake the dead.

Haven't they slept long enough?
Time to get them out of bed.

LETTER TO MY SON

Dementia runs in the family, so if I can't think of a name or a place, a moment everyone else can vividly recall, I feel afraid. Useless. Ashamed. You see, I don't want anyone to carry me into another room so I can get a view of a tree or remind me what a tree is or tell me what I'm sipping from is called a straw. I've seen it all before. My grandfather didn't know he was eating a banana—only that someone had to peel it for him, and that thing, that peel had to be thrown away. I'm not saying it's certain I will have dementia, but if I do, please know this: I won't be mad if you don't take care of me. I won't even know that you're not. Tell me everything's okay, and I will believe you. Tell me there's a bird on a branch outside my window, even if there is no window, and I will imagine he's singing to me. Once when a storm was coming my mother looked up at the sky, told me God was punching the clouds to make rain pour out. She never even believed in God. The point is this: I may not know exactly who you are when you come to visit. I may be confused. But when I hold your hand it will all come back in waves: rocking you in my arms when you were a baby, your little seltzer voice, my heart flooding my body with joy every morning you jumped in my bed. I will not be angry like some people with dementia can get. I've never been good at angry. I will not peel the yellow paper off the wall or bite my caregiver. Play a few rounds of blackjack with me. You deal. I will smile each time I get a picture card. Tell me I've hit twenty-one even if I bust. Use real chips, have party drinks with ice that clinks, a cocktail napkin with which to dab my lips.

LUNCHTIME STROLL

I could easily see my mind sliding
away. I stare for an hour at cherry
tomatoes growing in a stranger's
backyard, wonder how much water
these people have to give those
things, if they are ripe enough to eat.
I can't grow anything. I've tried. Even
the plants they say you can't kill,
I've killed. I don't recognize faces
anymore. It used to be names I couldn't
remember, but now it's faces, too. If I
walk into you on the street, even if I
know you but it seems I don't,
it's because I don't. Do not be offended.
Just help me find what used to be my
mind, when it was intact, whole, when it
could handle the news of the day. For now
I found an office chair in the alley which still
has some spring. You will find me rocking
back and forth, taking a memo. Look for it
in your inbox. It's a warning. It's a love letter.
It's all I have left.

Late September

7:11 p.m., dark again
as daylight, reluctant felon
turns itself in

We tread water at dusk
ask the moon to forgive us

remember when
we were about to begin

and spring broke out in a sweat
all of us on the steps
late evening sunsets
now a memory
as we ease into
the starched white pillow
of winter

This hurts my back,
my father would say
late July days at the beach
when he'd reach beneath the kelp
scoop us kids out of the ocean

We didn't care
about our father's pain
our mother's boredom
just wanted more
of the same—staying up late

party cake, loving the sun
for telling the moon to get lost
as we'd be tossed

by the waves
runaways, ice cream and sand
crusted between our hungry fingers

"WE ARE LIKE NO ONE ELSE IN THE WORLD,"

the killer's mother says
as she asks the victims to feel
her prayers

imagine her pain
looking at photos of the bodies
a dull knife
slicing into her belly

what song to sing
what blue sky
sweet air
can ever be hers
what's left
but to mourn
wish her son
was never born

if not for her
there'd be no baby
she held, comforted
fed with a spoon
no baby to turn

what poison
had she passed into her womb
the undecorated room
where his fingers grew long enough
to fit the trigger so well

what was she thinking
the day his brain formed
as he lay curled inside her
the time bomb gene
melting under his tongue

he could have been
my son

Completion

We like to cross things off our lists.
The wedding gift has been shipped.
Groceries in the fridge. Book written.
Dying is the last item to be checked off the list.
I wish I could cross it off myself as I was
in the act. I'd insert a pink ink cartridge
in my special Pilot, draw a withering line
through the word *die* (maybe a smiley face?)
as my last breath left my lungs. Be there for me
if and when, as I might need you to hand me
my pen. Hand me my pen.

Searching for Your Photo

for Thomas Lux

I look through every box
crammed with my son's old baby
pictures, family trips, soccer teams
all I want is to find that photo
of you, there were a few, that time
in Boston when you and others
came to visit, Charles Hotel, early
'80s, you were wearing that dumb
earring, even now from the beyond
you'd call it dumb, you who were once
so young, young until the day
you were no longer. The diamond
stud must have seemed cool.
I wanted to find that photo, you
laughing, sitting on the couch
we'd all been drinking, it was fun,
the only poetry was in our
hearts, this was just a visit, you were
no longer my teacher, now a friend
from the past. You called me fruitcake
and dummy so I knew you still
cared, me your student from long ago.
I wanted that picture to show the world
you being silly we were probably telling
bad taste jokes all of us stupid, all of us
together on the couch.

SUNBATHING ON TYRONE POWER'S GRAVE

Hollywood Forever, same cemetery as Fay Wray,
dangling like a scarf in King Kong's hand,
has-been swans, their screen days behind them,
float at the mouth of his grave.
Backs of my thighs burn on the stone, skin recoils,
sizzles, sinks into Hamlet's words, *Good night, sweet prince,*
And flights of angels sing thee to thy rest.
He dropped dead at forty-four, heart attack
fake sword fighting making a movie in Spain.
Nightmare Alley was our favorite—my dad's and mine,
saw it together on TV, he, too, had a heart attack at forty-four,
I watched him collapse on the living room floor,
Valentine's Day, I was 14, ran down 89th Street
yelling for a doctor. I love graveyards.
Would walk Mount Auburn Cemetery
outside Harvard Square with my old college professor,
big wool coats with pockets,
sometimes we could see the moon
in the afternoon, but we never saw the stars.
I left the cold winters back east, moved to LA,
wore a two-piece under my clothes every day,
you never knew who might have a pool.
A rotting corpse is teeming with life.
Maybe Tyrone's bones are still breathing today.
Maybe after my father's third, final heart attack

there was a moment he remembered only the good things,
whether or not they ever happened.
I used to sunbathe on Tyrone Power's grave,
when sunbathing was something we still did,
flowers around me, angels in bikinis smoking KOOL Lights.

BIOGRAPHICAL NOTE

Kim (Freilich) Dower, originally from New York City, received a BFA in Creative Writing from Emerson College, where she also taught creative writing. She has published three collections of poetry, all from Red Hen Press: *Air Kissing on Mars* (2010), which was on the Poetry Foundation's Contemporary Best Sellers list and described by the *Los Angeles Times* as "sensual and evocative . . . seamlessly combining humor and heartache"; *Slice of Moon* (2013), called "unexpected and sublime" by *O, The Oprah Magazine*; and *Last Train to the Missing Planet* (2016), "full of worldly, humorous insights into life as it is," says bestselling author Janet Fitch. Dower's work has been nominated for two Pushcart Prizes and has been featured in the Academy of American Poets' Poem-a-Day, Garrison Keillor's *The Writer's Almanac*, and Ted Kooser's American Life in Poetry, as well as in *Ploughshares*, *Barrow Street*, *Rattle*, and *Eclipse*. Her poems are included in several anthologies, including *Wide Awake: Poets of Los Angeles and Beyond* (2015) and *Coiled Serpent: Poets Arising from the Cultural Quakes & Shifts of Los Angeles* (2016). Kim teaches poetry in the BA program of Antioch University. She was City Poet Laureate of West Hollywood, California from October 2016 to October 2018.